Teaching Kids to Respect Others

REFLECTIONS, ACTIVITIES & PRAYERS ON BULLYING AND PREJUDICE

Kevin M. Dowd

TWENTY-THIRD PUBLICATIONS
twentythirdpublications.com

TWENTY-THIRD PUBLICATIONS
One Montauk Avenue, Suite 200
New London, CT 06320
(860) 437-3012 or (800) 321-0411
www.twentythirdpublications.com

ISBN: 978-1-62785-381-1
Library of Congress Control Number: 2018943222

Printed in the U.S.A.

A division of Bayard, Inc.

Dedication

For my mom and dad,
MaryAnn and John Dowd,
my first teachers in the faith
on the Feast of Pentecost, 2018

"Come, O Holy Spirit,
fill the hearts of Thy faithful
and kindle in them the
fire of Thy love!"

CONTENTS

INTRODUCTION

At a 2017 conference in St. Augustine, Florida, Bishop Felipe de Jesús Estévez spoke about growing up in Cuba, where the church was threatened by the Communist regime. In such dire circumstances, he said, the Vatican focused on two groups to ensure the survival of the church: the bishops and the catechists.

This book is meant for catechists in the broadest sense. Whether you are a parent or a priest, a Catholic school teacher or administrator, a teacher in a parish program, or a youth minister, there is something here for you. In whatever way you are called to share the faith and help form a new generation of Catholic Christians, I hope this book will help you in that ministry.

The particular theme of this book is respect. It is an elaboration of Jesus' call to love one another. At a time when bullying and cyberbullying are hurting so many young people, I hope that the ideas and activities in this book will help parents and teachers to shape young minds and hearts in ways that will reject bullying and embrace solidarity, community, compassion, and caring.

one

Praying to a Caring God

Can a mother forget her infant...?
Even should she forget, I will never forget you.

ISAIAH 49:15–16

REFLECTION FOR CATECHISTS

There is no greater gift we can give a child than to bring that child into a loving relationship with God. Our word *creed* comes from the words for *I give my heart*. Christian faith is about giving our heart to God. Relationship, of course, implies conversation; and with God, that conversation is prayer. Our culture, though, gives distorted images of prayer that could lead students away from belief in a caring God. If, for instance, they learn that prayer is like sitting on Santa's lap and making wishes, they will be disappointed when God says, "No" or "Not yet." If they think that prayer is magic, and that by saying the right formula or by praying hard enough they will get exactly what they want, they will be disappointed. "God is not a magician," Pope Francis has said. As adults, we have come to this understanding of prayer, but it is not obvious. It needs to be taught. Otherwise, atheists use the false understanding of prayer to "prove" to kids that "prayers aren't answered" and "there is no God." Giving our children a healthy understanding of prayer protects them from these assaults on faith.

APPROACHES

- Teach prayer as communication with God our best friend, who cares about every detail of our lives.
- Show students that God often answers prayer through people who are open to his will.

BIBLICAL ACTIVITIES

- Make fortune cookies with Scripture passages inside that express praise and thanksgiving to God. The Psalms are a great place to start.
- Reenact the miracle of the loaves and fishes. Be creative in what you use for bread and fish: donut holes, mini loaves of cornbread, Swedish Fish, Goldfish, etc. Most important, include in your script how Jesus told his Apostles to feed the crowd themselves. They didn't think they had enough, but once they let Christ work through them, there was more than enough! You might mention the African proverb: when you pray, move your feet.

CLASSROOM ACTIVITIES

- Play the Garth Brooks song "Unanswered Prayers" and discuss why Garth is happy. Lead students to understand that God always answers prayers, but not like a magician. There are no magic incantations that will compel God to give us what we want. Instead, God sometimes says yes, sometimes says wait, and sometimes says, "No...I'll give you something better. Trust me."

- Tell the story of St. Paul's "unanswered prayer" from 2 Corinthians 12:7–9. Explain that God is like a good parent who wants only what is good for us. Remember that God does everything out of love; and if something happens that is not truly loving, it is not God doing it.

SUGGESTIONS FOR FAMILIES

- Avoid saying "We have to pray really hard for..." as if "results" are tied to effort.
- As part of your evening prayer, have each person recount where they saw Christ during the day. Also, how did we allow Christ to work through us to care for others?
- When you pray the Lord's Prayer, teach what "Thy will be done" means. Give examples of accepting God's will.

PRAYER

Dear Jesus, help us to spread your fragrance everywhere we go. Flood our souls with your spirit and life. Shine through us and be so in us that every soul we come in contact with may feel your presence in our soul. **(St. Teresa of Calcutta)**

two

People Care and We Say Thanks!

I give thanks to my God at every remembrance of you.

PHILIPPIANS 1:3

REFLECTION FOR CATECHISTS

In her educational philosophy, Nel Noddings points to surveys in which students say nobody cares about them. As Christians, this should worry us. If students don't feel cared for, then we are not embodying God's very personal care for them. Noddings says that *being caring* is not enough; we must *create caring relationships*. This makes sense theologically too. God's care is always personal, always relational. It finds its clearest expression in this world through those who allow God to work through them, embodying God's unconditional love. In response, we say, "Thank you!" This gesture of gratitude completes the circuit of a caring relationship.

APPROACHES

- Teach that caring is daring! It is countercultural. Caring means putting people first, even when society says to put progress, profits, or popularity first. Caring involves an unselfish sacrifice of our time and energy.

BIBLICAL ACTIVITIES

- Ask students what they know about slavery. Do they know there are still slaves in the world today and that good people are working to free them? Then tell them about the runaway slave Onesimus. When St. Paul was in prison, he wrote a letter to Onesimus's master, Philemon, asking Philemon to free Onesimus. Use this story to discuss empathy, the Golden Rule, and ways empathy can be put into action to show we really care.
- Make faux stained glass windows to represent the Visitation. Discuss how Mary put empathy into action, emphasizing that Mary went "in haste" to visit Elizabeth and "remained with her about three months" (Luke 1:5–56), and also how Elizabeth showed gratitude. When someone does something caring for us, how can we let them know we appreciate it?

CLASSROOM ACTIVITIES

- Make little care packages for the caring people in students' lives, filled with Hershey's Hugs and Kisses and bearing tags that say, "I can tell you care about me. Thank you!"

- Introduce older students to the idea that caring is sometimes social and political. In this sense, people care about us through *solidarity* with us. Care is demonstrated by working for a better world: e.g., abolitionism; or the labor, suffragette, and Civil Rights movements; or Sr. Helen Prejean's anti-death penalty work, etc. Choose a class project to demonstrate your own care, not just in an interpersonal way, but as solidarity toward a better world.

SUGGESTIONS FOR FAMILIES

- Many people take care of us through services that often go unnoticed. Help children to have "eyes to see" by modeling gratitude toward garbage collectors, janitors, police officers, waitresses and waiters, farmers, and others without whose work we would be inconvenienced or in real trouble.
- When you go to Mass together, teach your children that *Eucharist* is a fancy word for *Thanksgiving*. Catholics don't celebrate Thanksgiving just once a year. No way! That's not enough for all the good things God does for us. Every time we go to Mass, we are there to say, "Thanks!" to God, who always gives the best gifts.

PRAYER

My soul proclaims the greatness of the Lord; my spirit rejoices in God my savior. The Mighty One has done great things for me, and holy is his name. **(Luke 1:46–49)**

three

We Care for Our Families

As for me and my household, we will serve the Lord.

JOSHUA 24:15

REFLECTION FOR CATECHISTS

The family—in all its different arrangements, from single moms and dads, to many generations living under one roof, to grandparents raising grandchildren, to the modern tradition of the nuclear family—is a critical place where we learn respect, caring, love, service, and forgiveness. As the Trinity is a perfect union of Love without losing the distinctions among the Three Divine Persons, so too the family should be a community of love where the diversity of the individuals is appreciated and nurtured. Strong families—always an ideal we struggle to attain—cannot help but overflow into the larger society, becoming sources of hope and healing.

APPROACHES

- When promoting love of family, be careful to avoid "family narcissism." Sayings like "family above all" and "blood is thicker than water" miss what Jesus wanted us to learn: that we are all one family, with God as Father of all.
- Christian life is a constant widening of the circle of those for whom we care. At first it is only ourselves. Next, it may be our own family. Then, the circle expands to include friends who are like us as well as those who differ from us. The circle grows even wider as we care for strangers. Ultimately, Jesus challenges us to expand the circle of love to include even our enemies.

BIBLICAL ACTIVITIES

- Read Matthew 12:46–50 together. Jesus uses the arrival of his family to teach about the family of God: "Whoever does the will of my heavenly Father is my brother, and sister, and mother." Have each child make a family tree that resembles an actual tree. Once all the trees are made, construct a giant tree and have students attach their own trees as branches. Each of our families is really just a branch on the family tree of God!

CLASSROOM ACTIVITIES

- Watch the musical ***Joseph and the Amazing Technicolor Dreamcoat*** together. Have a discussion about the things that tear a family apart (jealousy, lies, violence, etc.) and the things that bring it together (kindness, forgiveness, starting over, etc.).

- On St. Valentine's Day, make valentines for every member of the family. Be alert and open to non-traditional family structures, and be inclusive. On each valentine, have students write one thing they love about that particular person in their life.

SUGGESTIONS FOR FAMILIES

- Go to Mass each Sunday as a family. Make a tradition, like going out to brunch after Mass twice a month and discussing the gospel as it applies to your family and your values. On the alternate Sundays, spend the time after Mass doing service as a family for a food pantry/soup kitchen, homeless shelter, etc.
- On birthdays and Christmas, have family members choose one gift to give away to a person who has very little. Remind them that we don't give away our junk, which would mean we don't think very highly of the person we are giving it to, but we give things that are valuable, because when we give them to someone in need, we are also giving them to Christ.

PRAYER

Lord God, from you every family in heaven and on earth takes its name. Grant that love may prove mightier than all the weaknesses and trials through which our families sometimes pass.
(Pope St. John Paul II)

four

We Care for Our Friends

I have called you friends. **JOHN 15:15**

REFLECTION FOR CATECHISTS

Theologian Bernard Cooke noted that "Friendship is the primordial sacrament of God's love." Friends communicate God's own deep love for us through their presence and caring. At first a friend is just a playmate, but as kids grow they may encounter betrayal and manipulation. Aristotle spoke of three types of friends: those based on utility, pleasure, and the good. The rarest form of friendship is the third type, mutually wishing the good of the other. Aristotle considered this the perfect form of friendship because it was not a form of self-interest but a manifestation of genuine mutual caring. The friendship is deep and we sacrifice time and treasure for it—and even our life in the most extraordinary cases. Jesus is exactly this type of friend to us.

APPROACHES

- Discuss ways to detect when someone is using or trying to manipulate us. Let the young people know that betrayal by a friend can happen, and it is not a reflection on them but on the betrayer.
- Teach them that being loving doesn't mean being friends with everyone. Even Jesus walked away sometimes.
- Remind them that a true friend would never ask them to do anything bad and wouldn't want them to get into trouble.

BIBLICAL ACTIVITIES

- Tell the story of two of Jesus' close friends: Peter and Judas. How did Jesus feel being betrayed by Judas and having Peter deny that he knew him? What would be necessary to fix the friendships? Now tell them about one of Jesus' best friends, Mary Magdalene, and how she stayed faithful to his death. She was also the first witness of the resurrection!
- One of the great biblical stories of friendship is that of Ruth and Naomi. The friendship was so deep and full of love that both the reading and the musical version of "The Song of Ruth" are popular at weddings. Sing or listen to the song together and talk about why it is a fitting song for a wedding.

CLASSROOM ACTIVITIES

- Have each student make a step pyramid out of Styrofoam blocks. The top level with only one block represents the intimate friendship that reaches its pinnacle in married love. Explore the meaning of the various levels of friendship below the apex. Why does the pyramid get smaller as you move up?
- Brainstorm a list of things that destroy friendships, including selfishness, lying, stealing, rumors and gossip, cyberbullying, shunning, etc. Then use washed milk cartons to represent each vice, labeling each one with an item from the list. Have one volunteer stand at the front of the class. One by one, each student puts his or her carton in the volunteer's hands or arms. The volunteer has the job of not dropping a single one. Make sure that both hands as well as the arms are fully engaged in holding the cartons. Once the volunteer is fully loaded up with "vices," have the other students each walk up to him or her and try to shake hands. The volunteer is unable to shake hands and make new friends because of all the "vices." Talk about the meaning of the skit together.

SUGGESTIONS FOR FAMILIES

- Teach kids different terms for the associations they form, including acquaintances, playmates, classmates, teammates, friends, and best friends.
- All parents in the children's circle of friends might share their contact information with each of the children, having a joint talk about calling at any time in a bad situation. Providing options might make young people

(especially as they get older) more comfortable and likely to actually call an adult in a bad situation.

PRAYER

You have blessed us, O God, with the gift of friendship, the bonding of persons in a circle of love. We thank you for such a blessing.

("Prayer for Friendship" by Vienna Cobb Anderson, on www.beliefnet.com)

five

We Care for Our Teachers

"Do you understand what you are reading?"
He replied, "How can I, unless someone instructs me?"

ACTS 8:29–31

REFLECTION FOR CATECHISTS

In some cultures, teachers rank among the most important members of society, and have prestige and paychecks to match. Teachers in those cultures are highly respected for their work in sharing wisdom and knowledge and for contributing to the formation of healthy, well-rounded, successful, and mature members of the community. In our society, this is not always the case. Yet, as St. Luke emphasizes in the passage above, teachers of the gospel are critical in God's plan. Not out of self-interest, then, but out of a deep respect for the gospel itself, we do well to form young people who have Luke's *attitude of gratitude* toward religious educators.

APPROACHES

- Our values become most apparent in how we spend time and money. Our young people will learn quickly that we value religious education when it holds a secure place on the calendar and is not trumped by sports, sleep, social engagements, or anything else. Joining with other parents of all faiths, we can advocate for and create communities that respect the hours of religious education as sacrosanct.

BIBLICAL ACTIVITIES

- Have students, working in small groups and using smartphones or computers, look up and record occasions in which Jesus was described as teaching. Then, discuss the word *rabbi* and how much God values teaching and learning, considering that Jesus identified primarily as a teacher.
- Prepare a scroll ahead of class for a reading of the Great Commission (Matthew 28:19–20). In class, perform a dramatic reading. Discuss the meaning with the students. Then, hand out paper that has the semblance of a scroll, and ask the students to either draw or write ways in which they: 1. try to carry out Jesus' command in their own lives; and 2. have seen other people carrying out Jesus' command, being like Jesus the teacher. Gather the little scrolls around the large scroll in a display to celebrate teachers, teaching, and learning as Christ's followers.

CLASSROOM ACTIVITIES

- Do a mini-research project with students, learning about the various patron saints of teachers and of students. Make thank-you cards designed by the students with images or famous sayings of these patron saints, and address them to students' former teachers.
- One of the most moving stories of a caring student-teacher relationship is that of Helen Keller and Anne Sullivan. Disney filmed a television remake of the classic film ***The Miracle Worker*** in 2000. At 1 hour and 35 minutes, it is more suited to older students, but clips would intrigue younger students too.

SUGGESTIONS FOR FAMILIES

- In a hurried society, it is tempting to drop kids off and pick them up from a catechetical class and then speed off to the next activity on the agenda. Take time to speak with your child's teachers in front of your children, thanking the teachers for their work and dedication. This is a great way to model the virtue of gratitude.
- At family prayer time, be sure to remember religious education teachers.

PRAYER

Creator of all things, true source of light and wisdom, let a ray of your light penetrate the darkness of my understanding. Point out the beginning, direct the progress, and help in the completion. I ask this through Jesus Christ our Lord. Amen. **(St. Thomas Aquinas)**

Six

We Care for Our Community

How good it is, how pleasant,
where the people live together in unity!
PSALM 133:1

REFLECTION FOR CATECHISTS

Scripture talks about *me* getting to heaven, but also about us working for justice on this earth. Jesus taught us to pray "Thy will be done on earth as it is in heaven." If we forget the heaven part, we may form our students into great humanitarians without helping them to become disciples of Christ. If we forget the earth part, we may form spiritualists who don't value this earth enough to help bring about the kingdom of God here. In the balance between the two, we recognize that caring for the earth and working for justice are spiritual acts worthy of those on a pilgrimage to heaven.

APPROACHES

- As students get older, help them to identify not only personal sins, but social sins, which do so much damage to our community. They need to hear from the church, loudly and clearly, about the sinfulness of racism, sexism, destruction of the environment, and an economy that allows some people to live in luxury and to throw food away while leaving others to die from lack of basic needs.
- Some important skills to help students develop are active listening, dialogue, tolerance and appreciation for differences, and forgiveness. Having students summarize accurately another person's position in a discussion is a helpful way to teach the discipline of one or more of these skills.

BIBLICAL ACTIVITIES

- Read Matthew 25:31–46. St. Teresa of Calcutta said the poor were Jesus in his most distressing disguise. Make a collage of the many "disguises" of Jesus in our world today.
- Watch a video or a YouTube version of the parable of the good Samaritan. A lot of bullying happens in schools and online. Have students discuss the connection between what Jesus taught and our responsibilities when we see somebody bullied.

CLASSROOM ACTIVITIES

- Every major religion has some version of the Golden Rule. Have students take out their phones and do a mini-research project, working in small groups to find as many different versions as they can. Make posters, banners, or flags to represent this universal moral precept.

- Use different colored dominoes to represent various professions (blue for police, red for firefighters, white for health professionals, black for priests and religious leaders, etc.). Set up a fun dominoes toppling course and ask the students if it would work if you pulled all the blue dominoes out or all the red ones, etc. Remind them that we need everyone! Then, draw names from a hat to decide which student gets to knock down the starter domino. Post a video of it on the parish or school social media site.

SUGGESTIONS FOR FAMILIES

- Take family field trips to explore various vocations. Visit the police and fire departments. Take a trip to your capitol building and visit your representatives. Visit a farm, a fishery, and/or a fishing vessel. Tour a recycling center. Build on this list to create a unique itinerary. Make the connection to 1 Corinthians 12.
- Young people should recognize that we don't have "a garbage man" and "a lunch lady," for example. They are people with names. We know the principal by name, so we should also know the janitor by name and never just walk by, ignoring anyone as if they were invisible or unimportant.

PRAYER

Help us, Lord, to remember that whatsoever we do for the least of your brothers and sisters, we do for you. **(Matthew 25:40)**

Seven

We Care for People in Person and Online

The Lord appointed seventy-two others whom he sent ahead of him in pairs to every town and place he intended to visit.

LUKE 10:1

REFLECTION FOR CATECHISTS

The online world is filled with knowledge and possibility, but also with dangers and sin. Our catechesis should employ technology in the classroom as appropriate. We should also guide young people toward proper use of the internet and social media. As Pope Francis said, modern communication technology is "a gift of God which involves a great responsibility." Cyberspace is one of the places Jesus intends to visit (Luke 10:1). Our young people, in particular, are sent by Christ to be his presence there. It is part of evangelizing the culture, which Pope St. John Paul II spoke so much about.

APPROACHES

- The temptation to act differently in the online world, where anonymity masks identity, can be an important lesson about character and integrity.
- Help students to identify the "wolves" on the internet: inappropriate comments, character defamation and gossip, cyberbullying and other violence, pornography, identity theft and phishing, and other scams.
- Less obvious "wolves" should also be a part of our curriculum, such as addiction to video games and social media, and falling victim to impossible standards of happiness, beauty, and perfection.
- Be aware of the New Atheists, who see religion as a virus responsible for violence, oppression, and denial of human rights. YouTube videos, memes, and blogs are some of the ways they lure people away from faith. Sophisticated media evangelists like Bishop Barron and his Word on Fire ministry are a good resource.

BIBLICAL ACTIVITY

- Display a statue or icon of St. Stephen and tell the story of his stoning (Acts 7:54–60). Ask the students if they have ever witnessed someone ganged up on. Discuss motives and what to do. Then, turn their attention to the internet and social media. Do people get ganged up on there? What should they do if they see it happening? What should they do if it is happening to them? When a woman was about to be stoned to death, Jesus said to everyone there, "Let the one among you who is without sin throw the first stone" (John 8:7). The people dropped their stones and walked away. He saved her life! It takes courage to stand up against the crowd, though, so remind students of the "courage multipliers" (see chapter 17). Give each student a small rock, and tell them that these represent bullying and cyberbullying. Ask them to "drop" their rocks at the foot of the statue of St. Stephen if they reject bullying.

CLASSROOM ACTIVITIES

- Many police departments are willing to train faculty and/or students about online safety. Look into this training in your area.
- The YouTube video ***Dove: Evolution of a Model*** (1 minute 14 seconds) is a useful tool for showing how media images of beauty are distorted and lead to insecurities.

SUGGESTIONS FOR FAMILIES

- Delay the usage of smartphones and other portable internet devices by children until they are mature enough to handle the risks. Until then, allow them to use a family computer placed within a common area of the house. Use internet filters and monitor usage.
- Check out Stop Bullying, the U.S. government clearinghouse for information about bullying and cyberbullying (the website is: *https://www.stopbullying.gov/*).

PRAYER

Jesus said, "I watched satan fall from the sky like lightning. See what I have done, I have given you power." **(Luke 10:18–19)**

eight

We Care for the Sick

I was sick and you visited me. **MATTHEW 25:36**

REFLECTION FOR CATECHISTS

Sometimes people blame the sick for their illnesses. Think about lung cancer, diabetes, and HIV. When a non-smoker develops lung cancer, there may be more sympathy than when a smoker develops cancer. Similarly, when an HIV patient became positive through a tainted blood transfusion, there is often more sympathy than for an HIV patient who used drugs or engaged in risky sexual behavior. As Christians, we are called to be caregivers not judges. "If you judge people, you have no time to love them," said Mother Teresa.

APPROACHES

- Jesus healed people with his divine power. He expects us to use our own gifts to heal. These include ordinary things like visiting the sick, and professional things like working as a nurse/doctor or a researcher. They also include advocating for justice, such as providing adequate health care for all, and supporting international assistance organizations, such as Doctors Without Borders.

- For many students, sickness has already touched them in a personal way. They may have lots of questions such as: "Why did God let my grandmother die?" or "Does God make people sick to punish them?" Be prepared to answer the difficult questions around suffering, emphasizing that God is never the source of suffering and death. God is the one who will raise the dead to new life.

BIBLICAL ACTIVITIES

- Have students film a movie about one or more of Jesus' healing stories.
- Some biblical figures were *not* healed. Moses had a speech defect. Jacob had a limp. St. Paul complained of something that God would not heal that Paul called having "a thorn in my side" (2 Corinthians 12:7). We should never think that sickness and suffering are a good thing, but when we do suffer, we can offer it with Jesus on the cross. Set up a large wooden cross in class and use sticky notes to pin up the names of people God didn't heal or save from suffering and death, including especially Jesus. Include people from students' own lives. Discuss how Christians find hope in the resurrection and the promise of heaven, where "every tear will be wiped away" (Revelation 21:4) and death itself will be destroyed (1 Corinthians 15:26).

CLASSROOM ACTIVITIES

- Create a classroom skit about St. Francis embracing the leper, and then discuss how Christians should treat those who are sick.
- Watch a movie about St. Teresa of Calcutta (Mother Teresa) and have students write movie reviews or make movie posters.

SUGGESTIONS FOR FAMILIES

- Make posters representing each of the Spiritual and Corporal Works of Mercy, designed to fit on the vertical part of each step of your staircase (or make a staircase pattern out of the posters if your home has no stairs). Explain that we advance upward toward heaven by these practices. Remember to include the work of mercy added to the list by Pope Francis: care for creation.
- Don't be afraid to bring children to wakes and funerals, but take time to prepare them. Explain what will happen and assess and validate their emotions, which may range from fear and sadness to confusion and anger. Assure them that even though these are sad events, they are also important celebrations of a person's life on earth and prayers for their entry into heaven.

PRAYER

O Mary, intercede as our Mother for all the sick and for those who care for them! Grant that, through our service of our suffering neighbors, and through the experience of suffering itself, we may receive and cultivate true wisdom of heart! **(Pope Francis, Prayer on the World Day of the Sick, 2015)**

nine

We Care for Kids Who Are Bullied

A faithful friend is a sturdy shelter:
whoever finds one finds a treasure.

SIRACH 6:14

REFLECTION FOR CATECHISTS

Many websites give Bible verses related to bullying. Most of them suggest trusting in God and loving your enemy. These, of course, are good things. However, a young person might interpret Christian faith as requiring passivity in the face of the violence. Trusting in God is critical, but if young people have a magical understanding of God and prayer, their faith could be destroyed by God's seeming failure to intervene and bring relief.

APPROACHES

- Balance the "turn the other cheek" messages of Jesus with episodes of righteous anger, such as the cleansing of the Temple. Also, when the soldier slapped Jesus when Jesus was being questioned by the high priest, Jesus did not turn the other cheek. Instead he reproved the soldier (John 18:22–23).
- Instead of branding kids as "bullies," which then becomes self-fulfilling, we should offer counseling (perhaps professional help) while also challenging them to be the kind of person they are proud to be. Forgiveness and starting over must be part of the Christian message to our youth.

BIBLICAL ACTIVITIES

- Revisit the parable of the good Samaritan (Luke 10:30–37). Have the students re-imagine the story as a bullying parable. Put on a performance using Instagram or Facebook Live.
- For older students, tell the story of the woman caught in adultery (John 8:1–11). The goal is to evoke empathy, so at various points, ask how the woman must feel. Relate the story to students' lives by drawing parallels to those who are subjects of ridicule in person or online because of things such as their body size, being differently abled, being gay or lesbian, or being an immigrant or minority. Hand out paper and ask students to write, privately, the things they have seen, heard, experienced, or even engaged in that are bullying behaviors. Tell them not to censor it. Then, ask them to crinkle the papers into the shape of a rock. Explain that these are the rocks we use

today to destroy people. Place a basket at the front of the room and ask students to come up and drop their "rocks" in the basket if they are willing to reject these bullying behaviors and to stand up for others as Jesus did. (Read the papers after the class is dismissed. Be honest with students by telling them about this. I recommend reading them for two reasons. First, you will gain a better understanding of the violence that students experience. Second, you may find a cry for help.)

CLASSROOM ACTIVITIES

- Pray the Stations of the Cross, pointing out that Jesus did not carry the cross alone. If Jesus needed help and had support, then we will need help too. Whom can we reach out to? If we see someone else who is struggling, how can we be like Mary, Simon, and Veronica?
- Include bullying in your Examination of Conscience. Include sins of omission too: "Did I fail to help someone who was being bullied in person or online?" etc.

SUGGESTIONS FOR FAMILIES

- The nature of bullying is that it never "builds character" but instead tears someone apart, often leading to suicidal ideation and to permanent emotional scars. This is because bullying is: 1. violent (physically, emotionally, psychologically, etc.); 2. ongoing/repeated behavior (online it may be there 24/7); and 3. overpowering, such that the student cannot defend himself or herself.
- If children are bullied, don't blame them as if they are weak or brought it on themselves. Nobody deserves to be

bullied, and blaming the victim only compounds the problem and intensifies the pain. Instead, take their experience seriously, recognize what they are going through as a form of violence, and get them out of that violence.

PRAYER

Lord God, bless us with the courage to stand up for those who are bullied, and the grace to accept everyone as a brother or sister created in your own image and likeness. Amen.

ten

We Care for People in Every Country

The Lord said to Abram... "All the families of the earth will find blessing in you." **GENESIS 12:1–3**

REFLECTION FOR CATECHISTS

If our country becomes the primary object of our love, fidelity, and respect, it becomes an idol. God alone deserves that level of commitment and devotion. We are citizens of the kingdom of God, and our deepest loyalty belongs there. Love of country becomes the virtue of patriotism when it is an expression of love for God. It is not afraid of foreigners (xenophobia/nativism) nor is it puffed up with pride ("my country right or wrong!"). Instead, we humbly receive the gift of having this particular nationality, while equally recognizing the beauty of other cultures and lands.

APPROACHES

- Sporting events often promote patriotism as respect for the military and our veterans. This is an important aspect of patriotism. After all, "No one has greater love than this, to lay down one's life for one's friends" (John 15:13). Still, whatever serves the common good should be respected as patriotic service. By this wider focus, we avoid inadvertently promoting a militaristic view that is inconsistent with Christian ethics.
- We should balance "God bless America" with an understanding that God blesses all peoples and nations. Otherwise, we could be replacing the Christian understanding of God with a tribal American god.
- In every age, the least respected group of patriots are activists and protesters who challenge us to become "a more perfect union." Students should learn that patriotism includes the prophetic voice that refuses to accept injustices and calls us to provide "liberty and justice for all."

BIBLICAL ACTIVITY

- Have students build God's mountain (Isaiah 2:2–5) out of clay. To show that "all the nations will stream to it," use figurines holding flags to represent various countries, like the Opening Ceremonies at the Olympics. You might add animals to show that even natural enemies are now friendly on God's holy mountain.

CLASSROOM ACTIVITIES

- There is probably no better song to promote the authentic virtue of patriotism than "Finlandia" ("This is My Song"). Watch a performance of it on YouTube and go over the lyrics with the class.
- It is easy for students to strike up friendships with kids from other countries as they play video games together, or to form community around everything from music and sports to environmental and social causes. These friendships lead to a better view of the world, instead of seeing other countries as always desperate and inferior.

SUGGESTIONS FOR FAMILIES

- If it is within your means, travel to other countries. If not, take virtual tours and make lists or pin ribbons on a map of places you would like to visit. Keep learning together about new places, people, and cultures. Model respect for all people.
- Pray for our soldiers and also for the people of other countries who are suffering because of war and violence. Pray for peace, so children in every country can play and be happy.
- Pray an around-the-world Rosary together, where each decade is for the people on a different continent. (Use the five-continent categorization that the Olympic rings represent: Africa, Asia, The Americas, Europe, and Australia/Oceania.)

PRAYER

All the nations you have made shall come to bow before you, Lord, and give honor to your name. For you are great and do wondrous deeds; and you alone are God. **(Psalm 86:9–10)**

eleven

We Care for Immigrants and Refugees

You shall also love the resident alien, for that is what you were in the land of Egypt.

DEUTERONOMY 10:19

REFLECTION FOR CATECHISTS

A consistent message throughout the Scriptures is the commandment to take care of the stranger, the immigrant, and the alien. Abraham was called by God to become an immigrant. Biblical prophets and Scripture scholars alike interpret the story of Sodom and Gomorrah as a moral tale about the sinfulness of treating immigrant strangers with violence and contempt. After Moses led the Israelites out of slavery in Egypt, they were reminded by God: "You shall not oppress or afflict a resident alien, for you were once aliens residing in the land of Egypt" (Exodus 22:20). Jesus, whose family became refugees because of King Herod, told us that welcoming the stranger would be one criterion used in the last judgment (Matthew 25:31–46).

APPROACHES

- Talk about racism, xenophobia, and prejudice with kids. Help them to form consciences that refuse to see people as anything except brothers and sisters in the family of God.

- Engage the imagination and build empathy. What would it be like to leave your home, your school, your family and friends? What would it be like to make a journey where many have died on the way? How would you like to be treated in the new land?

BIBLICAL ACTIVITIES

- Make a well together in class or put a bucket on your prayer table. While gathered around the prop, tell the story of Jesus meeting the foreign (Samaritan) woman at the well (John 4).

- Make shields and decorate them with Christian symbols. Then, tell the story of Jesus' encounter with a military leader from the occupying country, Rome (Matthew 8:5–13). When the military man said, "Lord, I am not worthy to have you enter under my roof; only say the word and my servant will be healed" (Matthew 8:8), Jesus praised his faith. These are now the words we say just before receiving Communion. It is a way of expressing our faith, a faith that is like a shield protecting us from the devil and all evil (Ephesians 6:10–17). Even though the soldier was a foreigner, how did Jesus treat him?

CLASSROOM ACTIVITIES

- Have a refugee visit, or use a video such as ***Aya's Story*** from the U.N. (length: 2 minutes 49 seconds) *https://www.youtube.com/watch?v=dFqiYM2l9w8*.
- For a longer personal witness (34 minutes 39 seconds) about a young refugee from Iraq and Syria, watch Mario's story at *https://vimeo.com/262878648*.
- For younger kids, watch Grover from ***Sesame Street*** interview Tony Blinken from the State Department about refugees (length: 2 minutes 53 seconds) *https://www.youtube.com/watch?v=dUxKsG5YrPE* and then Google "Elmo and refugees" to find images of Elmo visiting with refugee children.

SUGGESTIONS FOR FAMILIES

- Contact Catholic Charities, Catholic Relief Services, or other agencies that help refugees and immigrants. Find out how you can help families locally or abroad. Check out CRS videos on YouTube as well.
- Learn the immigration background of your own family together.
- Check with your diocese to discover how many different languages are used to celebrate Mass. Then, join different ethnic communities for the Eucharist.
- Does your community have ethnic festivals? Take part! Go to the parades. Listen to the music. Sample the food. And most of all, meet people and start new friendships.

PRAYER

Lord Jesus, help us by your grace to welcome migrants and refugees with joy and generosity, while responding to their many needs. We praise you and give you thanks for the family you have called together from so many people. Amen. **(from "Prayer for Migrants and Refugees" by the USCCB)**

twelve

We Care for People with Different Skin Colors, Accents, and Cultures

Now there were devout Jews from every nation under heaven staying in Jerusalem...Each one heard them speaking in his own language. **ACTS 2:5–6**

REFLECTION FOR CATECHISTS

Racism is learned very early in life, and so we must be intentional about promoting respect for all God's people from the start. This begins with representing the diversity of God's creation in our classrooms through textbooks, posters and art, and, above all when possible, through meeting people of various backgrounds. Especially in communities that are ethnically homogeneous, the work to promote respect across ethnic and cultural differences is a critical component of Christian faith formation.

APPROACHES

- Thinking one's own way of speaking is normative is a form of supremacism. Exposing children to other dialects and accents through movies, music, and internet channels can help prevent this form of bias.
- While appreciating other cultures, be careful of tokenism and cultural appropriation.

BIBLICAL ACTIVITIES

- Research various cultural images of Jesus and Mary, and create a collage celebrating the universality (catholicity!) of God's love.
- Celebrate "The Days of Creation" by coloring and cutting out diverse images of God's creation, including the oceans and mountains, the sun and moon, dinosaurs and the whole evolutionary spectrum of land and sea creatures (this is important for showing that science and faith complement each other and that we don't read the Bible literally, even while we acknowledge that all of creation is ultimately God's doing). Include, especially, different skin colors, eye colors, hair colors, body sizes, ethnicities—all the diversity!—of humans. Inflate balloons with helium and attach one of these images to each balloon's ribbon tail while playing music to reflect the theme. By the end, the ceiling will be covered with balloons and the beautiful diversity of creation will be represented. Title this classroom art: "God said, 'It is very good!'"

CLASSROOM ACTIVITIES

- Obtain a copy of The Black Madonna icon and use it devotionally.
- Introduce critical reasoning about images. Ask, "Who are they forgetting and leaving out?" A lot of American and European religious artwork, for example, would lead one to believe that God is an old, white man, and that all the saints are white too.
- Sometimes, our good efforts have unintended side effects. Images of poor people, for example, might only portray black children in Africa or dark-skinned people in India or Latin America. Children might develop a sense of superiority, equating success and progress with their own ethnicity and country. Be intentional about introducing the beauty of other countries and the contributions made by people of all ethnic backgrounds.

SUGGESTIONS FOR FAMILIES

- Have images, books (including children's books), and movies about people from diverse backgrounds who respected the diversity of God's creation. Malala Yousafzai and Martin Luther King Jr. are great examples. Introduce your children to William Zdinak's painting "In His Image."
- Visit heritage sites that honestly and respectfully portray Native American history and the current situation. Don't shy away from tragedies like the Trail of Tears: children need to know how bad things are when we fail to love.

PRAYER

O God, you created all people in your image. We thank you for the astonishing variety of races and cultures in this world. Enrich our lives by ever-widening circles of friendship, and show us your presence in those who differ most from us, until our knowledge of your love is made perfect in our love for all your children; through your Son, Jesus Christ our Lord. Amen. **(from the *Lutheran Book of Worship: Minister's Desk Edition*)**

thirteen

We Care for Kids Who Are Differently Abled

Moses said to the Lord*: "O my Lord...*
I am slow of speech and slow of tongue."

EXODUS 4:10

REFLECTION FOR CATECHISTS

All children need role models, no matter what their abilities. The late Scripture scholar Fr. Daniel Harrington, SJ, found a hero in Moses. Dan was a lifelong stutterer. At age ten, he read in a newspaper that Moses had stuttered too. When he looked it up in the Bible, he found the passage above, confirming the speech defect of the greatest of Jewish heroes. From that encounter—seeing his condition reflected in the word of God—came forth one of the greatest biblical scholars of our age.

APPROACHES

- Use the term *differently abled* more than *disabled* to emphasize that every person's unique strengths and weaknesses are God-given and to be valued.
- "Not as people see does God see, because people see the appearance but the Lord looks into the heart" (1 Samuel 16:7). God often uses those whom the world thinks are less capable to do great things.
- Adapt the learning space, accommodate teaching techniques as necessary, and be sure students with wheelchairs, hearing aids, glasses, etc. are represented in the classroom (artwork, videos, readings, etc.) so everyone feels welcome.

BIBLICAL ACTIVITIES

- We often tell stories of Jesus' healings. Yet most people in Jesus' time and throughout history who had difficulties were not healed. It may be encouraging to kids, therefore, to hear stories of biblical heroes who were differently abled and whom God used as instruments of his grace *just as they were*: Moses was a stutterer (Exodus 4:10); Jacob limped (Genesis 32:32); Leah possibly had an eye problem (Genesis 29:17); Isaac went blind (Genesis 27:1); Saul was shy and moody (1 Samuel 10:19–23; 1 Samuel 16:14–18).
- Read Deuteronomy 27:18–19 and Leviticus 19:14 together. Ask students why what is being described is especially bad. What are examples today? What should we do if we see someone mistreating someone else?

- Read Luke 14:12–14 together. Ask students why Jesus taught us to invite those with special needs. How does it feel to be invited and included? How does it feel to be left out? What should we do if we notice that someone is being left out? Coordinate this together with a food drive or a visit to a soup kitchen.

CLASSROOM ACTIVITIES

- Inspiring sports stories are abundant on YouTube. For example, look up the stories of Jason McElwain, Jonathon Montanez and Mitchell Marcus, Jamarion Styles, Tatyana McFadden, and Chy Johnson.
- Sometimes, kids don't know how to interact with someone who uses a wheelchair or someone with autism, etc. Explaining the person's situation (or having them explain it if they choose), modeling appropriate behavior, and inviting students into friendship is key. Help them overcome possible fear and awkwardness to recognize we are all the same inside.

SUGGESTIONS FOR FAMILIES

- Be inclusive regarding invitations to birthday parties, sleepovers, etc. If you're not sure how to accommodate a child with a special need, reach out to the parents for advice and check out the WikiHow page on "How to interact with People Who Have Disabilities."
- Be alert to bullying. Young people with special needs are often targets. Teach your child to report bullying, to be a friend to those who are bullied, and to speak up if they are bullied.

- Read the book ***The Power of the Powerless*** by Christopher de Vinck for a wonderful, pro-life story of acceptance and love, endorsed by Mr. Rogers.

PRAYER

"Creator God, we are your people. We look to the future with optimism and with faith in You, as we pursue our call to provide justice and fullness of life for all people with disabilities. We pray that every man, woman and child may develop their potential and meet You in themselves and in one another. May we enjoy a totally welcoming community, with You as our center, joined hand in hand with our sisters and brothers. We ask this in Jesus' name. Amen."

(from *The Catholic Catalogue*, accessed at http://thecatholiccatalogue.com/prayers-for-persons-with-disabilities/)

fourteen

We Care for Gay People and Straight People

This is how all will know that you are my disciples, if you have love for one another. **JOHN 13:35**

REFLECTION FOR CATECHISTS

The topic of sexual orientation is difficult for many religious educators. Unfortunately, LGBT students are among the most consistently bullied. Even if they are not directly bullied, LGBT students are bullied indirectly by homophobic slurs when they hear a part of their identity used as a put-down. Surveys show that the church's advocacy for traditional marriage has been heard by a majority of people as a rejection of gay people. To overcome this perception, we must emphasize that every person is created in the image and likeness of God and is redeemed by Christ Jesus, in whom all divisions are overcome (see Galatians 3:28).

APPROACHES

- Emphasize that the church loves and accepts its LGBT members and requires everyone to treat gay people with "respect, compassion, and sensitivity," teaching that "every unjust discrimination in their regard should be avoided" (***Catechism of the Catholic Church***, 2358).
- Pope Francis, like our students, has gay friends, such as Yayo Grassi, whom he visited in 2015 when he came to the United States. Previously, the pope said: "A person once asked me, in a provocative manner, if I approved of homosexuality. I replied... 'Tell me: when God looks at a gay person, does he endorse the existence of this person with love, or reject and condemn this person?'..." He also said, "If someone is gay and he searches for the Lord and has good will, who am I to judge?"

BIBLICAL ACTIVITY

- Read Luke 6:36-42 and incorporate the two bullet points above in a discussion about the dignity of every person, gay or straight. Make a list of various forms of "unjust discrimination" that must be avoided.

CLASSROOM ACTIVITIES

- Celebrate the God-given dignity of each person in a birthday-themed prayer service. Decorate the classroom like a nursery with pink and blue balloons and streamers. Have cupcakes that are also decorated in baby colors. Set up a prayer table with baby bottles. Label each bottle with a description of a newborn baby, such as "a Black/White/ Latino/Middle Eastern/etc. child," "a gay boy/lesbian girl," "a child with autism," etc. Announce: "Today, we celebrate every birthday in the world ever! God is the Father of all, so we begin by praying 'Our Father...'" Tell the students that each bottle represents a baby loved and created in the image and likeness of God. Remind them that every child is equal and a reason to celebrate. Each child reads the description on a bottle and everyone responds by saying, "Happy birthday! Thanks be to God!" At the end, read Psalm 139:13–17 and let the birthday party begin!

- Turn a large poster of Jesus into several puzzle pieces. On each piece, write a descriptor such as "Asian people," "Arab people," "Black people," "Gay people," "Senior citizens," "White people," "Homeless people," "Poor people," "Straight people," etc. Talk about St. Paul's description of the church as the body of Christ. Build the puzzle together. Ask what would happen if we left a group out. Finish by reading 1 John 4:11–12, 20–21.

SUGGESTIONS FOR FAMILIES

- Read the USCCB document ***Always Our Children***. In it the bishops remind us that "God does not love someone any less simply because he or she is homosexual."
- In the same document, the bishops reaffirm: "The teachings of the Church make it clear that the fundamental human rights of homosexual persons must be defended and that all of us must strive to eliminate any forms of injustice, oppression, or violence against them." Especially important for young people, in light of bullying situations, the bishops "call on all Christians and citizens of good will to confront their own fears about homosexuality and to curb the humor and discrimination

that offend homosexual persons. We understand that having a homosexual orientation brings with it enough anxiety, pain and issues related to self-acceptance without society bringing additional prejudicial treatment." Modeling this level of respect begins in the home with how we treat and speak about gay children, relatives, friends, and people in general.

PRAYER

O Lord, it was you who formed my inward parts; You knit me together in my mother's womb. I praise you, for I am wonderfully made. Wonderful are your works. **(Psalm 139:13–14)**

fifteen

We Care for Those Who Are Hurting and in Need

Whatever you did for one of these least brothers or sisters of mine, you did for me. **MATTHEW 25:40**

REFLECTION FOR CATECHISTS

Pope Francis has repeatedly decried what he calls "the globalization of indifference." In the midst of our own comfort and busy lives it is easy to overlook the plight of people around the world. When Congress earmarks funds for people suffering in other countries, there is often a backlash from some Americans who think we should take care of our own first. If we make donations as private citizens to relief organizations, we may give only from our excess. Yet Jesus praised the widow at the Temple who gave a mere two coins because they were all she had (Luke 21:1–4). What Jesus praised in the widow is difficult for us to do, even heroic. Still, as one pastor put it, "Just because what Jesus said is difficult doesn't mean we can pretend he didn't say it."

APPROACHES

- Teach about the Real Presence in both the Eucharist and the church. St. Augustine said, "Receive what you are..." Why do we receive Christ? It is for the forgiveness of sins and for our salvation; but also for mission—to be Christ's presence in the world. In St. Augustine's words, "become what you receive."
- Our young people need to see that we help because love compels us, not because it makes us look or feel good. We don't do it for rewards or out of fear of punishment. We do it out of love.

BIBLICAL ACTIVITIES

- Help students realize that illness, tragedy, poverty, and other misfortunes are not God's punishment. Although sin has natural consequences and hurts us, our community, and our relationship with God, God does not react to sin by bringing evils upon us. One Bible story that makes this point well is the story of the man born blind (John 9:1–41). It is also a story that lends itself easily to a skit.
- Jesus said, "Whoever gives only a cup of cold water to one of these little ones to drink because he is a disciple—amen, I say to you, he will surely not lose his reward" (Matthew 10:42). The Station of the Cross in which Veronica wipes the face of Jesus is a touching example of providing comfort to someone in pain. Using white fabric napkins (or good quality paper napkins), have students create their own "veils" by drawing the face of Jesus. Ask students: how can we wipe the face of Jesus today? Have students encircle their image of Jesus with the words,

"Whatever you do for the least of my people, you do it for me" (Matthew 25:40).

CLASSROOM ACTIVITIES

- Become pen pals with residents of a local nursing home. Arrange for visits a couple of times a year. Write cards, create artwork, and perform music and dance for the residents.
- An important element in Christian discipleship is sacrifice. We cannot truly love without it. Give students opportunities to sacrifice. Perhaps they donate their snacks to a food pantry. Or, they could sacrifice recess time to work on fruit baskets to give to sick members of the community.

SUGGESTIONS FOR FAMILIES

- Read together Matthew 6:1–4 and James 2:14–17 and talk about the importance of putting our faith into action. Make a list of ways your family can serve others, and place a reminder of these ideas on your prayer table or refrigerator.
- After receiving Communion, talk about its meaning. Talk about ways to let Jesus work through you. Is anyone in need that you can help? Is anyone being bullied that you can stand up for and befriend? Is anyone left out that you can include?
- Make bookmarks with words often attributed to St. Teresa of Avila: "Christ has no body now but yours. No hands, no feet on earth but yours." (Alternatively, decorate your bathroom mirror with these words.)

PRAYER

Lord, make me an instrument of your peace. Where there is hatred, let me sow love. For it is in giving that we receive; it is in pardoning that we are pardoned; it is in dying that we are born again to eternal life. **(from the "Prayer of St. Francis")**

Sixteen

We Care for People from Different Religions

I have other sheep that do not belong to this fold.

JOHN 10:16

REFLECTION FOR CATECHISTS

At Vatican II, the bishops taught about our relationship with non-Christians in the declaration ***Nostra Aetate*** (1965). "We cannot truly call on God, the Father of all, if we refuse to treat in a brotherly way any man....The Church reproves, as foreign to the mind of Christ, any discrimination against men or harassment of them because of their race, color, condition of life, or religion" (NA, 5). Our love and respect flow not from imagining all religions as the same and equally true, but from a deep faith in God the Father of all, in Christ the Savior of all, and in the Holy Spirit, who is always at work bringing unity and love even outside the bounds of the visible church.

APPROACHES

- The ***Catechism of the Catholic Church*** teaches us: "Those who, through no fault of their own, do not know the Gospel of Christ or his Church, but who nevertheless seek God with a sincere heart, and, moved by grace, try in their actions to do his will as they know it through the dictates of their conscience—those too may achieve eternal salvation" (CCC, 847).
- The bishops at Vatican II extended their teaching to atheists and agnostics as well: "Nor does Divine Providence deny the helps necessary for salvation to those who, without blame on their part, have not yet arrived at an explicit knowledge of God and with his grace strive to live a good life" (***Lumen Gentium***, 16).
- In a mixed-religion environment, students might have questions and doubts. It is important for them to know that these are not sins. God gave us intelligence, and Catholics hold that faith and reason work together in bringing us to God. We should embrace our students' questions and doubts and help them to wrestle honestly with them.

BIBLICAL ACTIVITY

- During the Week of Prayer for Christian Unity (January 18–25), use Mark 9:38–40 and Ephesians 4:1–6. Make crosses from popsicle sticks and write "CHRISTIAN" on the vertical post, setting the first "I" at the intersection, so that on the horizontal post can be written "UNITY." Attach colored streamers, each one having the name of a Christian denomination. Add hearts to the streamers to symbolize unity in love. Use the words of Jesus in John 17:20–21 to pray together for unity.

CLASSROOM ACTIVITIES

- If kids hear about Islam only related to terrorism, they will have a warped view of Muslims. Likewise, there is a danger in Christianity of painting Jews as enemies of Christ. Be intentional in confronting stereotypes and bigotry. Teaching about other religions—showing them in their best light, the way we would want Christianity to be taught—does not undermine Christian faith, but deepens it.
- Learn about the celebrations of other religions as they occur. During prayer time, ask God's blessing on those from other religious traditions on their holy days.

SUGGESTIONS FOR FAMILIES

- Krister Stendahl coined the term "holy envy" to describe our appreciation of others' faith. Does Muslim prayer five times a day evoke a deeper commitment to prayer? Do the family rituals of Jews, such as the Passover Seder, inspire us to have our own family rituals? Modeling respect for people of other faiths can lead children to greater appreciation of their Catholic faith.
- Catholics believe that not every "religion" or spiritual force is benevolent. Modern satanism is easily found on the internet, and markets itself as humanistic and ethically superior to Christianity. Some atheists militantly attempt to destroy faith. Finally, some "spiritualities" are nothing but self-help therapies that are dangerously

narcissistic. Follow the church's lead and avoid the occult, ouija boards, mediums, and fortune tellers. Foster devotion to guardian angels and archangels, and prayer for the dead with the mind of the church instead.

- Watch Pope Francis' plea for interreligious dialogue. The video (1 minute 31 seconds) is embedded in the story here: *https://www.catholicnewsagency.com/news/in-first-video-message-pope-francis-stresses-unity-we-are-all-children-of-god-39381*.

PRAYER

How good and how pleasant it is, when brothers and sisters dwell together as one! **(Psalm 133:1)**

Seventeen

We Care Enough to Speak Out and Stand Up!

There is an appointed time for everything...
a time to be silent, and a time to speak.

ECCLESIASTES 3:1, 7B

REFLECTION FOR CATECHISTS

Silence allows bullying to persist. Adults frequently do not know what is taking place, though most students are aware. As bystanders, students often don't know what to do. If they speak up, will it make things worse or will they be targeted? If they tell a teacher, will everyone call them a rat, a snitch, or a tattletale? Even students who are bullied feel the pressure of this code of silence. If they ask a teacher for help, will they be seen as weak? Will adults help or will they just make everything worse? Add to this the confusion young people have regarding secrets, and we can see the need for good instruction. Young people need to know when to keep a secret and when to tell an adult. They need strategies for finding the courage to speak out.

APPROACHES

- Standing up and speaking out against bullying are obligations of baptism into Christ's prophetic ministry. These virtues transfer to adult life, where the need for voices against oppression and injustice is vital.
- Sometimes young people ask for help only to be told they need to develop a thicker skin or to stand up for themselves. These messages shut down communication and convince a young person that no one can help. They may become hopeless and feel helpless, two of the precursors to suicidal ideation.

BIBLICAL ACTIVITIES

- Distribute French fry trays to represent "papyrus and bitumen" baby baskets. Tell the story from Exodus 1:6—2:10 of how Pharaoh's daughter saved Moses, a foreign baby, from death. Say something like: "These baskets are a reminder that we must help people in need. Pharaoh rejected the Jewish baby boys. In our school and online, sometimes people are rejected too. They are treated badly or bullied. When we do that to someone, we are like Pharaoh, but God wants us to be like Pharaoh's daughter. In silence, think about whom you can help out." Conclude by filling the baskets with "baby Moses" treats to enjoy, such as Sour Gummy Babies.
- Retell the story of Joseph (Genesis 37). When the brothers plotted to kill Joseph, only Reuben stood up and spoke out. What effect did this have? Does one person's voice matter? How can we find courage to speak out when the whole crowd is saying something different?

CLASSROOM ACTIVITIES

- Conduct a lesson on secrets. Sometimes sharing something private is destructive and sinful, including internet posts meant to embarrass. However, when someone's life or well-being is at stake, we must tell the secret to a trusted adult.

- Standing up against a crowd can be difficult. We need courage multipliers such as:

  1. ***Prayer.*** God will give us courage. It is one of the gifts of the Holy Spirit.

  2. ***Partners.*** There is strength in numbers. Students commit with their friends to stand up together against bullying. Jesus sent his followers out in pairs (Luke 10:1). He knew they would be like "lambs in the midst of wolves" (Luke 10:3). Partners would help them to have courage.

  3. ***Practice.*** Imagining situations (role playing/making mini-videos) gives students practice and potential scripts to follow, which also multiplies courage.

SUGGESTIONS FOR FAMILIES

- Avoid saying, "Don't be a tattletale." This might encourage non-communication. Instead, explain the difference between things that should be kept secret and things they should tell a trusted adult.

- Beware of bullying masquerading as comedy. Bullying is not funny. Our humor at home has the power to communicate important values. Talk to the TV in front of your children. Whenever you see disrespect, stereotypes, or lack of representation, say it out loud so that your children learn to see and value diversity too.

- When we are told about a child being bullied, we often don't know how to respond. We worry that we'll over- or under-react. We wonder if the child is assessing the seriousness of the situation correctly. For help in understanding how to respond, visit: *https://www.stopbullying.gov/*.

PRAYER

Father of all, help us to hear your word and to act with courage: "Open your mouth on behalf of the mute, and for the rights of the destitute; Open your mouth, judge justly, defend the needy and the poor!" **(Proverbs 31:8–9)**

eighteen

Sometimes Some People Don't Care

A man fell victim to robbers...
[two leaders] passed by on the opposite side.
LUKE 10:30–32

REFLECTION FOR CATECHISTS

Some of our young people may be experiencing harm or abuse. They may have reached out for help and been neglected, disbelieved, or given insufficient assistance. An unhealthy spirituality based solely on the Suffering Servant can exacerbate the problem by making it seem that they are supposed to "carry their cross" because this suffering is God's will. This is wrong. There are things we cannot change, and then we have to "carry our cross," but when we can reach out for help, we should. Even Jesus had Simon of Cyrene.

APPROACHES

- Teach the Great Commandment as implying love for oneself in a healthy way.
- Children should know it is okay to sometimes feel bad, angry, sad, or unhappy. Faithfulness to God does not require a perennially happy attitude. False smiles are masks that can hurt us.

BIBLICAL ACTIVITIES

- John 8:1–11 is the account of the woman caught in the act of adultery. Jesus saw that the woman was ganged up on, and he saved her. Kids should know that Jesus cares and wants to save them too. However, Jesus works through people. Students know that sometimes people gang up, in person and online (cyberbullying). When we turn to trusted adults who can help us, we are turning to Jesus. And when we stand up for those being bullied, we are allowing Jesus to work through us. Paint rocks with a cross and the words "John 8:7" and stack them around the prayer table as a reminder to refrain from "casting the first stone."
- Make gingerbread churches! Each child should include a picture of him/herself as part of the decoration. This leads to the passage from St. Paul: "You are the temple of God…" (1 Corinthians 3:16). Asking for help when anyone is harming us is an important way to protect the body that God gave us as a dwelling place for the Holy Spirit.

CLASSROOM ACTIVITIES

- Read ***Alexander and the Terrible, Horrible, No Good, Very Bad Day*** by Judith Viorst. Have a conversation along these lines: Sometimes we have bad days and it seems like nobody cares. That is normal. But what about when it isn't just one day? What if somebody is doing something bad to you almost every time you see them? Maybe they tell you to keep it secret. That isn't normal. In that case, we should talk to an adult we trust and tell them what's happening. If the adult doesn't take you seriously or doesn't help you, go to another adult you trust. And don't stop asking until someone helps you.
- Older elementary school kids can learn from the book and movie ***Wonder*** by R.J. Palacio about a boy born with a facial deformity. Discuss how the main character, August, finds strength when people don't care about him.

SUGGESTION FOR FAMILIES

- The "sticks and stones" saying is unhelpful. Words do hurt sometimes! With boys, we tell them, "Be a man." With girls, we say, "Be a strong woman." This invalidates natural emotions, shuts down communication, and teaches kids to deal with problems by becoming callous. Instead, encourage them to be strong when it is appropriate and possible, to ask for help when needed, and to talk about what is happening in their lives without fear that we will judge them weak or a failure to their gender.

PRAYER

Say to the Lord, "My refuge and fortress, my God in whom I trust." He will rescue you. For he commands his angels with regard to you, to guard you wherever you go. **(Psalm 91)**

nineteen

Sometimes We Fail to Care

Have mercy on me, God, in accord with your merciful love.

PSALM 51

REFLECTION FOR CATECHISTS

We know our kids, like us, will sometimes fail to be loving and caring. Teaching them to recognize sin, to confess it, and to make amends is an important part of Christian formation. Bullying is a sin, but it is important not to label a child a "bully," which establishes itself in their minds as an unshakable part of their identity. Christianity represents opportunities for starting over. It represents finding ways for reconciliation and restorative justice.

APPROACHES

- We want young people to know that sometimes good people mess up. It doesn't mean that they are "messed up."

- Apologies can be very powerful when they are sincere. When adults force an apology, however, it is not helpful.
- Reconciliation and restorative justice take work. Children who have been involved as perpetrators or victims of bullying cannot simply become friends. Compare it to domestic violence. Imagine having the offender and the victim sit down together at lunch every day. Yet some adults impose this kind of "solution" on kids, which often only makes things worse.

BIBLICAL ACTIVITIES

- Make comic books that tell the story of Peter's denial of Jesus. Begin with Jesus' prediction, and end with Peter's reconciliation with Jesus.
- Imagine the story of St. Paul's conversion as a modern-day event. Have students design "Instagram photos/stories" and screenshots of the texts going back and forth between the Apostles. Saul's conversion was genuine, but the Apostles weren't sure. In the end, they forgave him and accepted him. This parallels our own stories. When someone hurts us and then seems to be friendly again, how do we know they are sincere? Should we trust them right away? How is trust rebuilt?

CLASSROOM ACTIVITIES

- Design paper cups with the words, "Sometimes falling into a hole is a chance to grow." Discuss the Apostles' failures, as well as other saints. Being human means that sometimes we fall into a hole. Ask the students: How can we turn a failure into a chance to grow? Complete the activity by talking about God's grace being like good soil. Fill the cups with soil and plant seeds together. Then, take care of them and watch them grow!

- Healthy guilt arises when we act sinfully. There is also such a thing as unhealthy guilt—when we feel bad even though we did nothing wrong. Offer concrete examples. Staying away from someone who hurts us is a smart decision, even if it seems unloving. There is no reason for guilt. Avoid adults you don't know, even if they seem to need help. Another adult will help them. There is no reason to feel guilty. Telling a teacher about something bad that another student is planning might make you feel like a tattletale, but it is the right thing. There is no reason to feel guilty. Have students give examples of healthy versus unhealthy guilt.

SUGGESTIONS FOR FAMILIES

- Sometimes words, actions, and failures to act can do harm that we can't fix. For example, we can't take bullying back, and we may really hurt the other person. They might keep hearing our words in their heads or see them like a permanent record on the internet. Two activities to help teach this: 1. squirt all the toothpaste out of a tube and then try to get it all back in; and 2. scramble an egg and then try to unscramble it.
- Take children to confession from time to time, and model going to confession yourself. Allow them the choice, though, whether to confess. Teaching them sincerity will foster a better appreciation for the sacrament.

PRAYER

Turn away your face from my sins; blot out all my iniquities.

(Psalm 51)

twenty

God Always Cares!

Do not fear...I have called you by name: you are mine.

ISAIAH 43:1

REFLECTION FOR CATECHISTS

When children are bullied, they may pray to God to make it end. If that prayer isn't granted, they may not only continue to suffer the bullying but also lose faith and hope. Forming students with a healthy understanding of prayer is essential. We don't want them to think of God as a magician, as Pope Francis warns us. We cannot force God into action by praying hard enough or by using the right words and formulas. Moreover, although God sometimes performs miracles, God usually works through people and through ordinary means. This is why students should learn to turn not only to God, but to the community God gave us. At the same time, while prayer will not typically end bullying on its own (because God does not typically violate human freedom), it is a source of strength and comfort. Spending time with God in prayer strengthens our relationship with God and makes us more like Christ. This is the real purpose of prayer.

APPROACHES

- Discourage a Santa Claus image of God who keeps a list of when we are naughty and nice and decides whether we are worthy of our requests.
- Discourage a candy machine or magic understanding of prayer in which paying the right amount or saying the right formula automatically leads to getting what you want.
- Foster a sense of prayer as relationship. The question "Does prayer work?" then becomes silly. We wouldn't ask if a relationship with our grandparents "works." It is the relationship that matters, not what we get out of it.

BIBLICAL ACTIVITIES

- Ask students if they have ever written a note on their hands so they don't forget it. Some people go even further and have a tattoo to remember a loved one who died. God goes even further still. Read Isaiah 49:15–16 with the students. Our names are engraved on God's hands! Have students trace one of their hands on colored paper and cut it out. Invite them to write their names on the hands and decorate them, assembling them onto a bulletin board emblazoned with the words from Isaiah. Talk about the Eucharist as one way that God shows that we are never forgotten! God is always there for us, listening, loving, and leading us to help others.
- Invite parents to a reenactment of the Last Supper. Broadcast it on social media live as well. Make the connection between the Eucharist and the washing of the feet (John 13:1–17). Jesus expects his disciples to be his

presence in the world, humbly serving others, being the answers to prayers.

CLASSROOM ACTIVITIES

- Put together a PowerPoint slide show of ways the class has been the body of Christ in the world today through humble service. Set it to a musical version of the saying, "Christ has no body on earth but ours..."
- Learn "The Servant Song" to help catechize students. Check with the pastor to see if students could sing the song at Mass.

SUGGESTIONS FOR FAMILIES

- Share the story of the man who drowned because he was waiting for a miracle instead of seeing that God sent him plenty of rescuers: *https://catholicexchange.com/hearing-god-speak*.
- Explain the both-and approach of Catholics to prayer. We pray for healing *and* we go to the doctor, because God usually works through people. We pray for help getting through a difficult time *and* we ask for help from others. We pray for those who are hungry *and* we donate food and work at soup kitchens, because God also works through us.

PRAYER

By this everyone will know that you are my disciples, if you love one another. **(John 13:35)**

Other Titles in This Series

Teaching Kids to Care for God's Creation

Reflections, Activities and Prayers for Catechists and Families

MARY ELIZABETH CLARK, SSJ

Based on Pope Francis' *Laudato Si'* (*On Care for Our Common Home*), this book presents 30 well-designed lessons on learning what we can do—in the classroom, in the home, and in the community—to raise awareness and take action to ensure that our planetary home will be sustainable for future generations. The prayers and reflections in each chapter help us make care for the Earth part of our faith and spirituality.

80 PAGES | $9.95 | 5½" X 8½" | 9781627853408

Teaching Kids to Care

Reflections, Activities and Prayers on Practicing Virtues

SR. JANET SCHAEFFLER, OP

From alphabets of courtesy to gratitude trees, here are hundreds of activities, conversation starters, and suggested Scripture passages that encourage caring. Organized by 25 virtues—compassion, empathy, justice, and more—this essential resource also includes brief reflections and prayers for each virtue. The ideas and approaches can be used at home, in classrooms, or in small or large groups to help children of all ages grow into the compassionate and caring people God created them to be.

80 PAGES | $9.95 | 5½" X 8½" | 9781627852524